Printed in Great Britain. For information address
Harper & Row, Publishers, Inc., 10 East 53rd Street, New York,
N.Y. 10022.

Library of Congress Catalog Card Number: 77-5213
Trade ISBN 0-06-022222-0
Harpercrest ISBN 0-06-022223-9

First American Edition

Printed in Great Britain by Cox and Wyman Ltd, London, Reading and Fakenham

*Anita Harper and Christine Roche are both members
of the Kids' Book Group, a collective of women
writers and illustrators.*

How We Live

by Anita Harper

with pictures by Christine Roche

of the Kids' Book Group

Harper & Row, Publishers

New York, Hagerstown, San Francisco, London

People live in all kinds of places.

Some people live in houses.

Some people live
in boats or trailers.

Or apartments or rooms.

Some people live with their friends.

Some people live alone.

Some people live with their family.

Some people live in orphanages.

Some people live with just their Mum.

Some people live with just their Dad.

Some small families live in big houses.

Some big families live in small houses.

Some people stay in the same place all their lives.

Some people keep moving.

Some people like where they live.

Some people hate where they live.

Some people have nowhere to live

even though many houses remain empty.

People live everywhere.